JESUS, MY SON

JESUS, MY

SON

Mary's story

told in poetry and art

by Helen Rayburn Caswell

JOHN KNOX PRESS
RICHMOND, VIRGINIA

Library of Congress Catalog Card Number: 62 – 19203

to my daughter, Mary

JESUS, MY SON

I

Where did you put the little earthen cup?
I'd like to hold it in my hands a while—
ah, thank you, John.

                  Oh, go ahead and smile
and shake your head at an old woman's whim.
I know you hold that other cup more dear!
But only once he drank from it the wine
that stood for sacrifice and blood. From mine
he drank cold water as a little boy.

Smooth-polished by his hands, it speaks of joy
and not of blood. It speaks to me of him
who was my child, a long, long time ago.
Cool to the touch it is, filled to the brim
with light.
       The other cup's the world's, my dear—
my memories are in this small one, here.

II

Ah, John, how quickly has the time gone by!
How thin and white my hair; how full of years
this body! And my face! It brings to mind
a creek bed when the summer rains have past!
Like summer rains, once on a time, my tears
fell passionately, showered warm and fast.
Not any more. What earthly use have I
for wasteful tears, who am about to die?
For age, no tears. For age, remembering
of moments like tall mountains standing clear
of clamoring small things that make a life.
And oh, the memories I've kept apart!
The things I have to ponder in my heart!

III

The thing I best remember is the light.
That day the angel came, the light was there.
It filled the room so suddenly I might
have thought the sun uncovered by a cloud,
except the sky was cloudless, hot and bright.
It was the kind of light a rainbow brings.
I stared out at the rooftops, wondering,
and heard the voice, like distant thundering.
You've heard the little locust, when he sings?
Strange, the immensity of little things,
sometimes. The voice was never very loud,
but as the locust's song fills up the sky,
it filled the room, just as the light had done.

The light and sound and presence were the same.
And this strange sound, this voice, called out my name.
I turned and saw him, standing at the door,
bigger than anyone I'd ever seen before,
bigger than anyone or anything.
At least, he seemed so, dressed the way he was,
in all that white and gold with blue, and light
behind and all around and even through him, much
the way the sun shines through the leaves in spring.
He said to me, "Hail, Mary, favored one!
The Lord be with you!"
                              I was terrified.
I was so frightened that I could not speak.
My mouth was dry with fear; my legs were weak.
And as I trembled there and stared at him,
he told me gently not to be afraid.
He told me then that I would have a son
and call him Jesus, and he would be great.

My son would be the king, on David's throne,
and reign forever.
                    Foolishly I said
the first thing that came into my reeling head.
"How can this be?" I asked, "I know no man!"
Then such a look he gave me, and he said,
"The Holy Spirit will come unto you;
the power of the Lord encompass you.
Your child will be the Holy Son of God!"
He told me of Elizabeth, my kin,
and of the boy child that she soon would bear.
I heard the words. I tried to take them in,
and in my heart began a wordless prayer
for understanding.
                    All at once, the light
seemed entered into me. I felt it sing
along my nerves; I felt it in my throat
and deep inside, and light and words were one.

A warmth, a song, a melting, thrilling thing . . .
I don't know how to tell you what it was,
but down I went upon my knees, and wept,
the hot tears coming quickly to my eyes.
"Behold the handmaid of the Lord," I whispered.
"As you have said, so let it be with me."
Then he was gone; the light alone remained,
slanting like sunset on a dusty day,
and it was slow to go, just as his voice
was lingering when he was long away.

Yet when a day or two had passed, it seemed . . .
I don't know . . . something that I might have dreamed.

IV

My first thought then was for Elizabeth,
old woman that she was, and she with child,
and right away I went into the hills
to where she lived, in case she needed me.
That's what I told myself. That's what I said,
but it was I had need of her, instead.
Fifteen I was, and both my parents dead.
Elizabeth was great with child, but looked
much younger than I had remembered her.

As we embraced, I felt the tiny shock
of movement as the babe within her leapt.
My cousin laughed. The sudden tears of joy
ran down her wrinkled cheeks, and then she cried,
"This is a blessed day I've lived to see!
The mother of my Lord has come to me!"
And do you know, my cousin saying that
made it seem real and true to me at last.
I felt such love and thankfulness to God
as I had never known before. My soul
began to sing, quite of its own accord,
a psalm of praise.

     But John, I could not see,
and still cannot, after these many years,
of all the maidens, why did God choose me?

V

No, John, that isn't so. Whatever else,
I know what I was not. Now, looking back,
I know. I was so very human, John,
and simple, and a prey to all the cares
of human, simple people.

                      You don't know,
for instance, how things were when I returned
to Nazareth from Juda. Three long months
I had been gone. The child within me showed,
a fullness visible beneath my shawl,
and Joseph . . . Oh, I never shall forget
the way he looked at me! That he would doubt
my word had not occurred to me at all.

Yet it was natural to disbelieve,
and he was kind. He would have done the thing
in secret and would not have had me stoned,
but I was sick with worrying. You see?
How little faith I had?

                        That very night,
the angel came to Joseph in a dream.
Dear Joseph! He would never doubt a dream!

VI

The light was there again in Bethlehem
when he was born. It was a lovely night.
I can remember how the stars came out
as we drew near the inn, and how the moon
shone on the grass that blew along the slopes
and waved like water in the evening wind.
I can remember, if I shut my eyes,
the pungent smell of oxen in the cave,
the plaintive sound the little donkey gave.

Mehetabel. That was our donkey's name.
It must have seemed a strange and foreign place
to poor Mehetabel. It did to me!
So very strange, that nothing was quite real,
the town, the inn, the dry and ancient cave
where cobwebs hung, bespangled with the chaff
of years, and least of all myself. I feel
again, now, thinking back to it, the pain
that crept upon me, stifling and strong,
and growing through the hours of the night
until I was no longer anything
but pain. Then, in its last extremity,
it changed. I felt within me all the power
that ever was, a surging song of strength,
relief and tenderness. And all around,
the light was shining. Cobwebs turned to gold,
and golden chaff lay drifted on the ground.
There was no corner of the cave left dark.

The door was open to the evening air
and on the hillside, light shone everywhere,
brighter than any moon, brighter by far
than sun at noonday, or the brightest star.
And while the brilliance shone, I felt a glow
of joy, but as the light began to go,
I had a vague presentiment, as though
the happy time were past, and ever more
a nameless dread would wait outside my door.
Perverse, in one so singularly blest.
They brought the child and put him at my breast
where he lay quietly and gazed at me
with cloudy violet eyes.

                            What did he see,
I wonder, such a solemn little face!
Did he feel alien in such a place?
Out in the meadows, shepherds saw the light
and angels told them that the Christ was born.

They all came crowding in, at break of morn,
to see the baby, lying in the hay.
And some knelt down to worship him and pray,
and others looked, and laughed, and went away.

VII

John, have I ever told you what he said,
that strange old man who came and took my child
and held him, in the temple? That first time,
it was, when we had taken turtle doves,
and were presenting Jesus to the Lord.
He spoke as one who knew us. At the last,
he looked at me through tears that veiled his eyes,
and said, "A sword shall pierce thy own soul too . . ."
Oh, he was right, John. What he said came true!

VIII

A few had taken what the shepherds told
as notable. It was a different thing
when wise men from the east came seeking him
who was to rule the Jews, to bring him gold
and frankincense and myrrh. They were so grand,
you know, and strange and foreign-looking, too,
that all the people hung on every word
they said. At last the king, old Herod, heard.
That night my husband had another dream,
and woke from it with sweat that wet his brow
and eyes that stared about him wild with fear.
Nothing would do but that we all get up
and flee, that very instant, for our lives.

A year we spent in Egypt, one whole year,
so far from all our friends and kin and dear,
familiar Galilee. I thought at first
it was perhaps a needless thing to do.
But then one day a caravan came through,
and people told us of the massacre
of all the little children under two.
Oh, John, it makes me weep, even today.
A woman never mothers only one,
but must lament for every mother's son.
So when I thought of all the babies dead
and mine alone alive, I bowed my head
to thank the Lord, as Noah's house had done
after the deluge. But I found that I
was not like Noah, on Mount Ararat.
I could not thank God for a thing like that.

IX

Those were the best years, there in Nazareth,
and so they passed the faster. Busy years,
with children being born and growing up,
and never time for worrying or fears.
I wasted all that precious time, I think,
preoccupied with unimportant things.
Or maybe not. For who can judge the good
of laundered linens, songs a mother sings,
a loaf of bread, a toy from scraps of wood?
And all the things I never thought to say . . .
I think perhaps he heard them anyway.

X

But it was hard, you know, to keep in mind
that he was different, my first-born son,
he that I nursed and he whose swaddling clothes
I changed. He seemed the same as anyone.
As on that day when he could not be found
among the caravan. As last resort,
we went back to Jerusalem, and there,
before the rabbis in the temple court,
we found him. Oh, the weak relief I felt!

I had been frantic! And I told him so,
in front of everyone.

              With some surprise
he looked at us and said, "Did not you know
that I must be about my Father's work?"
As though, if I had known, I'd not be fretting.
I *did* know, really, but I kept forgetting.

XI

When Joseph died, my eldest was a rock
to lean against, and we all leaned on him
those years he kept the shop and stayed at home.
It was a calm and peaceful interim
before a storm.
                    My old, vague fears returned
the day I saw my cousin's son, young John.
He that I felt leap in his mother's womb
now looked no longer young, but gaunt and wan,
half starved from living in the wilderness,
and dressed in skins. Wild. And his eyes were wild,
baptizing men and preaching everywhere
that our Messiah was my first-born child.

XII

From that time on, my son was not my son.
It was not only that he went away . . .
It was, oh, something else. We could not talk.
I never could find anything to say.

There was one time, just at the first, I tried
to keep him by me, at my beck and call,
to prove it to myself and show them all,
whatever happened, that he still was mine.

It was in Cana, at a wedding feast;
they had run out of wine.

                          I did not see
what he could do about it, but I asked.
Not for the bridegroom or the bride. For me.
How gently then he told me how it was,
"Oh, woman, what have I to do with thee?"
Yes, then he made the water into wine
the guests all praised as being very fine.
I would not know, for as I raised the cup,
tears filled my throat. I could not swallow mine.

XIII

The pomegranate dropped its orange bells,
the olive ripened and along the hills
windflowers cast their seeds and died and then
winter was over and they bloomed again.
Like windflowers, words on the winds came through,
to whip about the streets of Nazareth,
words of my son. Words of such wondrous things
and terrible, which ones could I believe?
So, with my younger sons, I went to see,
to find out for myself what things were true.
He was at Peter's house, and all the town
were crowded in the court. We could not pass,
and sent word through to Jesus that we'd come.

He did not pause, but stretched out either hand
above the crowd, and we could hear him say,
"These are my mother and my brethren,
who hear the word of God, and do his will."
He did not come to us.
                              We went away
with heavy hearts. We did not understand.

XIV

Spring came again, and in the wilderness
acacia blossomed gold. The apricots
grew ripe and full, fell softly to the ground,
but every day was dark with dreariness.
I knew what was to come, or thought I knew,
and yet I did not know. What had gone wrong?
What of the wise men and the angels' song?
The throne of David?

                       Passover approached.

Again I journeyed to Jerusalem,
for I was done with waiting and with yearning,
and I would go, though there be no returning.

XV

As I went through the town, I heard the truth
from strangers, from the crowds that filled the streets
and surged, a moving wall, behind the cross
that showed above their heads. I wept, I pushed,
but other women pushed and many other
women there were weeping. No one heard;
no one believed that I was Jesus' mother.
How long we struggled up that narrow street!
But when at last we came out on the hill
and I could see him clearly, it was worse.

His naked, bleeding body haunts me still.
My hands reached out, but could not take the thorns
from that dear head that had lain on my breast.
My arms ached for the cross he had to bear,
but could not help him, could not give him rest.
I would have dashed the hateful vinegar
onto the ground and given him good wine,
but even that I could not do for him.
He was the crowd's; he was no longer mine.
Then lightning lit his face and I could see
his eyes. My son was looking straight at me.
Remember, John, how much his eyes could say?
When he was just a little boy, sometimes
they widened with an anxious, wondering love.
That was the way he looked at me just then,
as he had looked once, as a little boy,
so full of hurts, I thought my heart would break.
Yet in his pain, he worried for my sake.

For then he said, "Woman, behold thy son,"
and gave me over to your keeping, John.
Yes, he had seen the torn place in my soul
and tried with his last breath to make me whole.
Through tears I looked, despairing, on his face,
and knew that none could ever take his place.

XVI

The light was gone; it had gone out with him.
That afternoon upon the skull-shaped hill
night came too early, and there were no stars.
Never had evening been so dark and chill.
Never had sabbath dragged so gray and still.

Then at the third day's dawning I awoke
to hear the song of spring the swallow sings,
and as we crossed the quiet, sleeping town
the kind of golden light a rainbow brings
lit up the east, and touched the cypress trees
and gilded crocus growing on the hill.

It shone upon the stone that stood apart,
and in the empty tomb shone brighter still.
I did not see the truth of it at first.
I had not ever thought of it before.
But now my heart groped haltingly ahead
toward a beckoning and light-filled door.
Then as I stared, I heard the angel's voice,
"Fear not, for he is risen, as he said."
The linen clothes lay in the sepulcher,
but he had gone. My Jesus was not dead.

XVI

He was the light, and lingered here a while,
a brightness in the night, to show the way.
Without the light then would we reconcile
ourselves to death, as to the end of day.
We were the earth-bound, but the light is free.
It has no bounds nor bonds and neither earth
nor death may hold it fast. Thus will it be,
that man will hear about the wondrous birth,
and man will see the brilliance from afar.

He'll follow, worlds and centuries apart,
the shining of a distant, gleaming star
to find the light bright-burning in his heart.
    And I? All that I've lost I treasure still.
    God ever needs an empty cup to fill.